BARBARA BUSH

OTHER BOOKS BY LOUANN ATKINS TEMPLE IN THE BIOGRAPHY FOR BEGINNING HISTORIANS SERIES

George W. Bush

Laura Bush

Lyndon B. Johnson

George H. W. Bush

Lady Bird Johnson

BARBARA BUSH

A Biography for Beginning Historians

LOUANN ATKINS TEMPLE

THE LBJ FOUNDATION

Distributed by the University of Texas Press

First edition, 2025

♾ The paper used in this book meets the minimum requirements of ANSI/NISO Z39.48-1992 (R1997) (Permanence of Paper).

Library of Congress Cataloging-in-Publication Data

Names: Temple, Louann Atkins author
Title: Barbara Bush : a biography for beginning historians / Louann Atkins Temple.
Description: First edition. | [Austin] : The LBJ Foundation and Briscoe Center for American History, 2025. | Includes bibliographical references. | Audience: Ages 8–12 | Audience: Grades 4–6
Identifiers: LCCN 2025012383 (print) | LCCN 2025012384 (ebook)
ISBN 978-1-4773-3205-4 paperback
ISBN 978-1-4773-3206-1 pdf
ISBN 978-1-4773-3207-8 epub
Subjects: LCSH: Bush, Barbara, 1925–2018—Juvenile fiction | Presidents' spouses—United States—Biography—Juvenile fiction | Women—United States—Biography—Juvenile fiction | LCGFT: Biographies
Classification: LCC E883.B87 T46 2025 (print) | LCC E883.B87 (ebook) | DDC 973.928092 $a B—dc23/eng/20250520
LC record available at https://lccn.loc.gov/2025012383
LC ebook record available at https://lccn.loc.gov/2025012384

doi:10.7560/332054

In memory of
Jo Anne—
a lover of biographies

CONTENTS

BARBARA BUSH

INTRODUCTION

"One morning in September I turned on the television and suddenly realized that, with the exception of Arafat, I knew every single person personally that I had seen on the tube during that hour. That's the life that George Bush has given me. Amazing life. Lucky, lucky me." Barbara Bush wrote those words late in life.

She appreciated that she had lived a big life and a good life. She had grown up in a world where she was cared for and comfortable. She had married the first man she loved, and they remained devoted to each other for seventy-three years until her death. She had been First Lady of her country. She had traveled the world. She had contributed in major ways to the well-being of her fellow citizens.

Indeed, she had endured tragedy in the death of her daughter Robin when the child was three years old. She had also lost her fifty-three-year-old mother suddenly in a car wreck. She had known the fear of having her fiancé missing in action in World War II. She had suffered depression as an adult, not sure of where she fit in the world. She had despised the roughness of a political world she could not hide from.

She had been forced to move twenty-nine times and essentially start over again each time.

Yet, whatever the difficulty, Barbara weathered it all and could say, at age seventy-nine, “Amazing life. Lucky, lucky me.” You are about to go on a roller coaster ride.

CHAPTER 1

BARBARA BUSH AS A PERSONALITY

Barbara Bush is known as much for her one-of-a-kind personality as for her singular accomplishments. She needs some explaining because, although she was uncomplicated, there were many sides to her.

First, what she was not: She was not cerebral. She was bright but saw the world from a practical, not academic, point of view. And she was emotional, as was all the family. "We cry when we are glad," she said, "*and* when we are sad."

She was not glamorous, nor did she want to be. She wore conservative clothes in solid colors and three strands of fake pearls. The *Washington Post* said her popularity as First Lady was "in no small measure a byproduct of the appearance of a woman on the center stage who dared to look her age."

She was not manipulative. She expressed her opinions strongly and directly but never tried to maneuver her way into getting what she wanted.

What made her angry: self-importance, unfairness, unkindness, and criticism of her family. She heard a lot of that in politics, and she ran from it. If an interviewer asked her a barbed question, her answer was likely to be a curt "Next?" or "No comment."

How she ran her life: in a practical, organized, efficient manner, getting things done and quickly moving on. In her many house moves, she never left still-packed boxes in the garage. Without delay, she put everything away, got out the backyard grill, and returned to a settled life.

Her passions: family and friends; dogs; reading; her volunteer work with a focus on literacy; participating in sports, especially playing tennis and swimming; gardening; needlepoint; traveling; entertaining.

The traits that always served her well: her sunny disposition; her easy way of making friends; her physical energy and persistence; her ability to bounce back from disappointment; her appreciation of both everyday life and exotic adventure—whatever was handed her.

The trait people loved or feared: her feisty humor, which was ever-present, always blunt, sometimes knife-edged. She was quick to apologize when she realized she had hurt with her quips.

The bottom line: A compassionate heart guided her.

CHAPTER 2
CHILDHOOD

On June 8, 1925, Barbara Pierce was born into the safe and stable world of her parents Marvin and Pauline; a sister, Martha; and a brother, Jim. The family lived in Rye, New York, a town of eight thousand people who knew one another. Rye boasted one movie theater, a public library, a meat market, a bakery, and a greengrocer, but no full-service grocery store. Barbara's father commuted by train to New York each day, and her mother stayed at home to rear children and indulge her love of gardening.

Marvin Pierce was his daughter's hero. In one of her memoirs she called him "a smiling man." Thirty-one years old when Barbara was born, he was employed at McCall Corporation in New York, which published popular women's magazines. Later he became McCall's president and chairman of the board. He had known success in college as both a Phi Beta Kappa and an athlete and was a hardworking man. Barbara turned to him for attention and warmth and fun. From him, she learned to love sports.

Her pretty mother, less demonstrative than her father, spent much of her time caring for Barbara's brother Scott, who was born five years after Barbara with a cyst on the bone marrow of his shoulder that kept him in and out of hospitals for much of his childhood. Barbara described her mother as "an exquisite housekeeper" and as the one who "did most of the scolding in the family." She spanked her children, and Barbara, later, spanked hers also. Barbara learned from her mother her love of gardening and of needlepoint.

Slender sister Martha, five years older than Barbara, was known for her beauty. As a teenager, she was a model featured on the cover of *Vogue* magazine. By contrast, Barbara was large for her age—five feet eight and 145 pounds at age twelve. Barbara remembered her mother saying, at the dinner table, "Eat up, Martha. Not you, Barbara." As a child, Barbara idolized Martha, and as adults, they were close friends.

But Barbara was a little scared of Jim, the mischievous one, three years older. She irritated him when she tagged after him and especially when she went home to "tell" on him after he broke family rules.

Barbara tended to mother her younger brother Scott, who was sick for much of his childhood but grew up to be an excellent athlete. He was known in the family for his kindness.

Barbara's pleasant childhood in a three-story, five-bedroom brick house and a welcoming neighborhood included dogs and tree houses, jump ropes, bicycles, paper dolls, make-believe stories acted out with friends, listening to the radio, and playing tennis and swimming. At night everyone in the family read. This became Barbara's lifelong delight. Louisa May Alcott's *Little Women* was among her favorites. Most Sunday afternoons she went to the movies.

As a teenager, her life changed dramatically. At the age of fifteen, in her junior year of high school, she left home for a girls' boarding school in Charleston, South Carolina. At sixteen, she met her future husband.

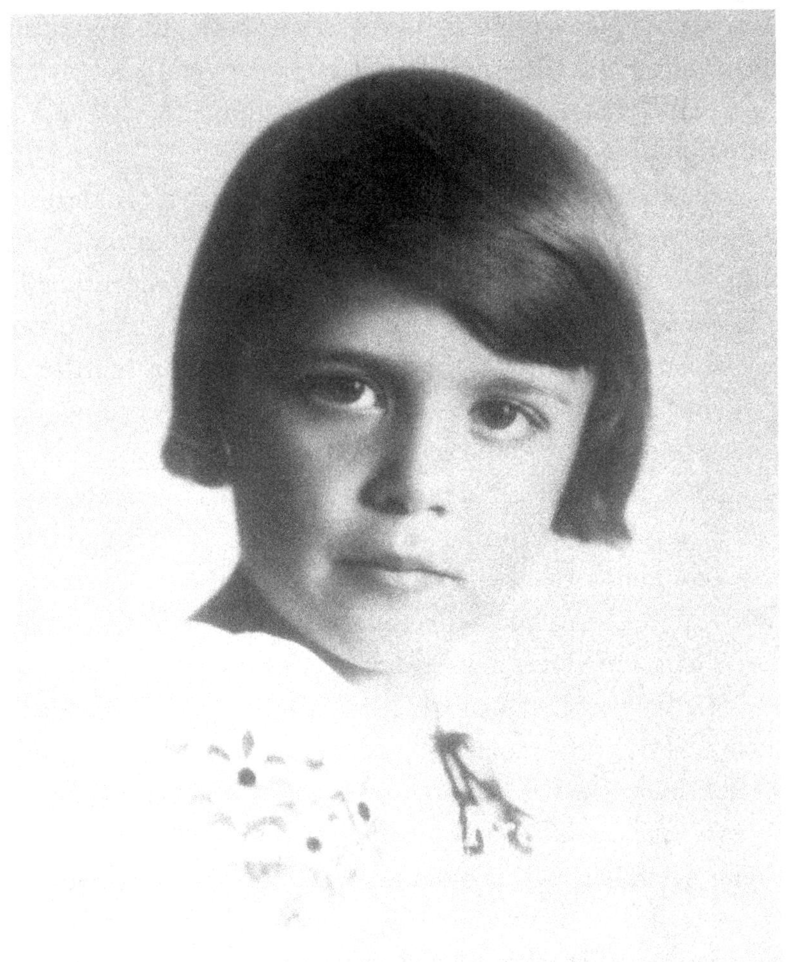

Barbara Pierce, age seven, around 1932. Courtesy of George H. W. Bush Presidential Library and Museum.

Barbara's sister Martha had attended Ashley Hall in South Carolina before Barbara because their mother wanted them to know different parts of the country. The school, near downtown Charleston, had expansive green lawns, huge oak trees, and traditional architecture in an oceanside Southern city conscious of its important roles in both the American Revolution and the Civil War. It had graduated another famous American—Madeleine L'Engle—the author of young adult books such as *A Wrinkle in Time.*

On the overnight train to Ashley Hall, Barbara left feeling lonely and empty, but when she arrived and began meeting her classmates, these feelings disappeared. "I felt miserable for about fifteen minutes," she said, "until I met some other girls." She was ready for this next step in growing up. All her life she benefited from moving swiftly into new experiences, many unanticipated and often jarringly uprooting.

Barbi, as her classmates called her, learned that she was in a conservative and formal setting. School rules dictated that girls could not wear makeup or nail polish, they could not go out with the same boy two weekends in a row, and they must wear hats and gloves and hose if they left campus.

She participated in extracurricular activities and especially liked the drama club, where she played everything from an angel in the Christmas pageant to Beatrice in Shakespeare's *Much Ado About Nothing*, a continuation of her delight as a child in acting out make-believe stories with friends. She excelled at swimming. Her classmates remembered that she knitted and that she was the one who ate the most hot biscuits at one meal without being caught by the faculty. By age fifteen, Barbara had cemented in herself interests and a personality that would accompany her for a lifetime—her enthusiasm for sports and for reading, her reputation as a jokester, her optimistic outlook, and her quickness to adapt to the new.

At Christmas of her first year at Ashley Hall, Barbara returned home, little realizing that she was about to meet George Bush, her future husband. The year was 1941. On December 7, Japan had bombed Pearl Harbor, and the United States had gone to war. That, too, would personally affect her in ways she could not imagine. Over the holidays, Barbara, wearing a new red-and-green dress, attended a teenage dance in Greenwich, Connecticut, near her hometown of Rye. A young man from Greenwich, George Bush (called Poppy), noticed her, what fun she seemed to be having, and asked to be introduced. They danced one dance and then sat out the next, chatting, because he did not know how to waltz. He told her he went to Phillips Academy in Andover, Massachusetts, and she said that she attended school in South Carolina, a thousand miles from Andover. He asked what she was doing the next night. They were both going to a dance in Rye. Barbara went home to tell her mother she had met the nicest, cutest boy, and George told his sister, Nancy, that he had met a wonderful girl who was beautiful and funny. Later, Nancy assessed his attraction by saying, "I think he saw a person sure enough of herself to reach out to others and not be worried about herself all the time. And they're much the same qualities that my mother had."

The next night, Poppy and Barbi had hardly begun dancing when her brother Jim annoyed her by cutting in on them. He wanted to meet George, who was known as an athlete, so he could ask him to play in a basketball game the following night. Poppy said yes, then asked Barbara if she would go out with him after the game. Romance had begun.

All too soon, the holiday ended, and they returned to their schools. They exchanged frequent letters, and she knitted him argyle socks. George invited her to Massachusetts to his senior prom, and she gladly traveled the long distance. It was her first senior prom and it included her first kiss. After the dance, she said, "I floated into my room and kept the poor girl I was rooming with awake all night, while I made her listen to how Poppy Bush was the greatest living human on the face of the earth."

In June of 1942, George graduated. Against his parents' wishes, on his eighteenth birthday, he enlisted in the Navy rather than go on to Yale, where he had been accepted and as his parents had expected.

That fall, when Barbara returned to school for her senior year, she stopped off in Chapel Hill, North Carolina, where George was in training. Other than that brief visit, they had only letters to sustain their romance. (And for a short while she had an alligator, which George sent Barbara as a gift. It ate the frog in her family's swimming pool, then disappeared into the woods.)

The next June, in 1943, Barbara graduated from high school in a class of thirty, and George got his wings, becoming the youngest pilot in the US Navy at that time. He had seventeen days' leave. His mother invited Barbara to join the family at their summer home in Kennebunkport, Maine. Barbara was scared. Would the family like her? She met them and was overwhelmed by their teasing of her and of each other. Quickly she realized that this was their way of having fun, and quickly, the Bush family took her to their hearts. Together she and George happily picnicked and played tennis, rode bikes, and walked on the beach. Always lurking in their minds was the realization that George was about to go off to war. By the end of the seventeen days, they had become secretly engaged—secret, George said, only to the extent that the German and Japanese high command weren't aware of it. Neither family was surprised, and both approved. Seventy years later the couple would still be vacationing in

Barbara Pierce in her late teen years, around 1944. Courtesy of George H. W. Bush Presidential Library and Museum.

Kennebunkport, now with their children, grandchildren, and great-grandchildren, just as they had been with George's parents and grandparents in 1943.

That fall Barbara went to Smith College (from which her sister Martha had graduated) in Northampton, Massachusetts, and George was stationed on an aircraft carrier in the

South Pacific, flying a torpedo bomber, which he named "Barbara." Before he left the United States, he presented Barbara with an engagement ring, a star sapphire that had belonged to his Aunt Nancy.

Barbara's interests at Smith were not academics but soccer, having a good time, writing letters to George, and reading and rereading the ones she received from him. Sometimes the letters arrived in stacks and, for some periods, did not arrive at all. One day she received one from a pilot in George's squadron saying that George had been shot down off the island of Chichi Jima, Japan, but that he had been seen swimming toward a raft. This pilot had strafed a Japanese boat heading for George's raft and alerted a submarine to find George and pick him up. There was hope that he might be safe. For three miserable, breath-holding days Barbara waited until she learned that George had floated on the ocean in the raft for three hours until the submarine had arrived and taken him, the only survivor of his crew, to Hawaii. From there he rejoined his squadron. Barbara later read in *Life* magazine that the Japanese from Chichi Jima had been known to practice cannibalism.

Soon George would be coming home, and they could marry. They had not completed their educations, but in the midst of World War II, many young people were unwilling to postpone marriage because it felt as if today was all they could count on. Barbara dropped out of school shortly after she had begun her sophomore year and started planning a December wedding. George was waiting for a military transport to bring him home from the South Pacific, making his return date uncertain. On Christmas Eve, he called from New York to say, "I'm home."

Immediately, they put already-made plans for their wed-

George and Barbara Bush on their wedding day, Rye, New York, January 1945. Courtesy of George H. W. Bush Presidential Library and Museum.

ding into operation. The invitations had been printed, and they only had to write in the date of the ceremony. On an icy January 6, 1945, nineteen-year-old Barbara walked down the aisle of the First Presbyterian Church in Rye before 250 guests, in a white satin dress and her mother-in-law's wedding veil.

Eight bridesmaids attended her in emerald green dresses, carrying red and white carnations, and wearing green ostrich feathers in their hair. George awaited her at the altar in his Navy dress blues. They partied with their guests, spent the night in New York City, and then boarded a train the next day to honeymoon at the Cloister, a resort in Sea Island, Georgia.

CHAPTER 3

MARRIAGE

George returned to duty, this time moving about the United States as his new squadron trained, with Barbara joining him whenever practical. For the next eight months, she learned to cook and clean in barely adequate apartments from Michigan to Maine to Virginia, all the while dreading his return to the war zone. But before George could be called back into duty, World War II ended on August 14, 1945, when President Truman broadcast on the radio that Japan had surrendered unconditionally. In the midst of the cheering and horn honking of celebration, Barbara and George stopped into a church to thank God and to pray for the many friends they had lost in the war. The Navy released George in September, and within days he began his long-delayed college education at Yale University in New Haven, Connecticut.

George went to class and studied and became a member of Phi Beta Kappa, the most prestigious academic honor society in the United States. He played baseball as captain of a Yale team that played in two college World Series, and he participated in campus activities. Meanwhile, Barbara kept house in a small apartment that shared both a kitchen and a bathroom with two other families. She played bridge, went to the movies, and worked half a day at the Yale campus store, selling books and clothes and even toothbrushes, with her black poodle at her side behind the counter.

Yale did not accept female students, and she chose not to finish her college education at another campus. She kept score for many of George's baseball games, standing behind the dugout, until the coach asked her to move behind a fence to avoid injury because she had become pregnant. After son George was born, she quit her job to concentrate on motherhood. In the coming years, Barbara could have returned to college with George's support. She chose, instead, to have a large family.

George rushed through school in just three years, earning a degree in economics. Eager for adventure and challenge and ready to be independent of their families, the Bushes headed for a place of which they had never heard rather than remain on the East Coast they knew. "I was young and in love and would have gone anywhere your father wanted," Barbara later told her children. The day after graduation, George drove his parents' gift to him, a new red Studebaker, two thousand miles south and west to Odessa, Texas, where Dresser Industries had offered him a job in its oil-related subsidiary. Barbara and baby George waited in Kennebunkport until he found them a "sorry little apartment" (as Barbara called it).

In this part of Texas, sand that sometimes smelled of oil swirled in the air, rain was rare, cactus substituted for trees and flowers, the land lay flat, and the sky spread vast—jarringly but intriguingly different from New York or Connecticut or Maine. Here Barbara felt as if she entered adulthood. "When you are a couple all grown up, nobody's son or daughter, nobody's shadow, you are you," she said. The Bushes fell in love with Texas, their new home.

They remained in Texas, except for one 9-month assignment in California, for the next eighteen years—a time of financial success and of entry into politics, a time when they established their family and made lifelong friends and put down new and deep roots. It also was a time of almost unbearable sadness.

The Bushes had hardly settled in Odessa before the company transferred them to California for those difficult nine months. George worked seven days a week, and the company moved them about to four different towns, causing Barbara to have to pack and unpack and learn her way around in a new place repeatedly. Two significant events occurred while they lived in California. Barbara learned that an automobile accident had killed her mother and put her father in the hospital. Her family decided that Barbara, who was seven months pregnant when the accident occurred, must not endanger her unborn child by making the hard trip home for the funeral. She had to grieve half a continent away from her father and siblings.

Soon, their daughter was born. They named her Pauline Robinson, after Barbara's mother, and they called her Robin for short.

Within a few months, Dresser Industries moved the family back to Texas, this time to Midland, twenty miles from Odessa. Midland, an oil boomtown, boasted twenty-one thousand people and 215 oil companies. There they remained for the next eight years. After having squeezed themselves into cramped little apartments in all their past moves, they bought their first house—bright blue—in a new neighborhood dubbed Easter Egg Row because each house was painted a different color. Midland life felt cozy, full of couples who were also newcomers to Texas and who also had families far away. They became family to each other, cooking together in their backyards and watching each other's children. Barbara taught Sunday school and volunteered at the hospital and the little theater. Family life and volunteer life were *her* life.

George's career expanded when he and his neighbor began a business as oil developers then expanded once again as they included two more friends and formed Zapata Petroleum Corporation. The family also expanded with the birth of their third child, John Ellis, called Jeb.

The year was 1953. When Jeb was a few weeks old, Robin, on waking one morning, said something unlike a healthy three-year-old: "I might go out and lie in the grass and watch the cars go by, or I might just stay in bed." Thinking Robin had a minor childhood illness, Barbara took her to the pediatrician. The doctor ran tests and then called Barbara and George into her office. She told them that Robin had leukemia, for which there was no cure, and that the child had only weeks to live.

George's uncle, a doctor at Memorial Sloan Kettering Hospital in New York, counseled that although no treatment then existed to save Robin's life, perhaps they could prolong it until some medical breakthrough would.

By nightfall, loving friends filled the Bushes' house, offering to help. The next day Barbara and George left their boys in the care of those friends and boarded a plane with Robin for New York.

For the next few months, Barbara remained in New York,

constantly at Robin's bedside, reading to her, playing with her, and helping her get through multiple medical tests and painful blood transfusions. George had to return to Midland to work. On weekends he flew to New York. One time the doctors allowed Robin to return briefly to Midland to be with her brothers. Eventually, however, the medicine became less effective, and Robin fell into a coma. Barbara and George held her at her death. Barbara combed Robin's hair one last time before she let her go.

Hoping to help other families, Barbara and George allowed doctors to study Robin's body before she was buried. In the meantime, the family held a memorial service in Greenwich, Connecticut, where George's family lived. The month was October. Barbara noticed the lovely colors of the fall leaves and how life goes on. As, indeed it did, with their two boys in Midland, to whom they now rushed home, knowing they had to tell this painful news to Georgie, who was only seven.

Again their friends attended them, but the adults were shy about mentioning Robin's name, fearing the pain it would cause Barbara and George. The family needed to talk about Robin, and Georgie finally made it easier for everyone with his innocence and frankness. At a football game, he stated, before several people, that he wished he were Robin. His father asked why, and he replied, "I bet she can see the game better from up there than we can from here." The adults learned from this child that talking helped.

Depression overcame Barbara. She woke in the middle of the night in physical pain. She leaned on George and wept in his arms. Her dark brown hair began to turn white even though she was still in her twenties.

Finally, she felt as if she had begun to live life again the day she overheard Georgie tell a playmate that he couldn't go to the friend's house because he mustn't leave his mother. "That started my cure," she remembered. "I realized I was too much of a burden for a little seven-year-old boy to carry."

Barbara and George took concrete steps to recover. They relied on their faith, without which, Barbara said, they could not have survived. They honored Robin by setting up the Bright Star Foundation to fund the study of leukemia. The family began a tradition; when they wanted to express their love for each other, they said what Robin had once said—"I love you more than tongue can tell." Barbara began working in the community again. And life did go on.

Neil was born in 1955 and Marvin in 1956. The family moved into a slightly larger house; they got a puppy. In the summers the children went to Camp Longhorn in Central Texas and the whole family to Kennebunkport in Maine.

One summer, driving home from Maine with three of her children and Otha Fitzgerald, the African American woman who worked for her, Barbara learned the realities of segregation in the South. Otha could not eat with them in restaurants or stay in the same hotels. They had to buy their food at a 7-Eleven and eat outside, and at night, Otha slept in the car. Barbara suddenly appreciated "how protected my life was and always has been—from such ugliness."

The Bushes had now lived in Midland eight years. With sadness and anticipation, they left what Barbara called "this cocoon of warmth and love" and moved on to Houston, on the other side of Texas, in order to be closer to the oil rigs George's company owned. Soon their daughter Dorothy Walker Bush (Doro), named after George's mother, was born. George had moved the family into a new house while Barbara was in the hospital. Trying to be helpful, he had unpacked and put their possessions in drawers, but he had done it without regard to where those possessions should be. Barbara found socks in the kitchen and measuring spoons in the bedroom. She re-sorted things for months. She was the organizer of the family.

Over the next years, she managed a household with five children, kept score at their baseball games (all four boys played), helped with homework, drove carpools, acted as Cub Scout den mother, disciplined misbehavior (her children called her the Enforcer), read books to the youngest at bedtime, kept a scrapbook of each child, and sewed felt sequined Christmas stockings for them. Jeb mused, as an adult, "I don't know how she did so much alone. Maybe there were two of her." Meanwhile, George traveled most of the week, and when he was home on weekends, they rarely went out except to go to church on Sundays. It was a focused life. Their household became slightly smaller when Georgie left for boarding school—Phillips Academy in Andover, Massachusetts—where his father had gone.

The Bush family (*left to right:* Jeb, Marvin, George, Doro, Barbara, Neil, and George W.) in front of the United States Capitol, Washington, DC, 1967. Courtesy of George H. W. Bush Presidential Library and Museum.

CHAPTER 4
POLITICS

Slowly, their lives began to turn outward again. Now politics filled their days. George had been successful in business and turned to the next challenge—getting elected as chairman of the Republican Party in Harris County. Barbara learned that opponents vying for political office could be mean rather than statesmanlike when she heard verbal attacks on George, and she discovered she would have to sit through speeches hundreds of times as she and George visited all 210 precincts. This, she said, was when she took up needlepoint, in order to endure endless speaking occasions.

George won the election. Next, he ran against Democrat Ralph Yarborough for the US Senate. Barbara campaigned hard, even walking from house to house at night to deliver political leaflets to people's front doors. The Democrat won, and Barbara learned the pain of being rejected by voters.

George returned to business until another opportunity came along, this time to run for a new congressional seat. In 1966 he became the first Republican elected to Congress from his county and one of only two in the state of Texas. The Bushes moved to Washington, DC. From military postings across the country to Odessa to California to Midland to Houston and now to Washington, Barbara had become expert at the complexities of moving: vacating one house and buying another, saying goodbye to friends, being the newcomer in town, packing and unpacking, finding new schools for her children, locating a compatible church, grocery store, cleaners, shoe repair, and pediatrician. She lived a life of constant readjusting.

In her memoirs, she called Washington life "exciting, overwhelming, intimidating, interesting, exhausting." Barbara and George attended big receptions and frequent black-tie dinners. They learned the distinctive protocols of the nation's capital, where women left calling cards when they visited and it was important to call people by their proper titles. She attended congressional wives' lunches and showed visiting Texans around the monuments and famous buildings. She also still drove carpools, worked in her garden, and played tennis. On weekends, George returned to Texas to talk to constituents, and Barbara took the children sightseeing in Washington. After George's reelection, she began writing a weekly column called "Washington Scene" for Houston newspapers.

Important history was made in those years. Civil rights bills passed; the Vietnam War raged; Martin Luther King, John F. Kennedy, and Robert Kennedy died at the hands of assassins; Richard Nixon won the presidency; astronauts walked on the moon.

In 1970 George ran again for the Senate and again was defeated, this time by Democrat Lloyd Bentsen. Soon after that, President Nixon appointed George as ambassador to the United Nations. (Barbara was in her mid-forties, and twelve-year-old Doro was the only child left at home.)

George and Barbara began the next breathtaking two years with a quick orientation tour throughout Europe to see UN agencies and meet dignitaries. They were the center of attention at each stop. Bands played for them as they got off airplanes, and fashion designers had showings for Barbara to see their clothes.

They arrived back in New York and moved into the official residence of the US ambassador, an apartment at the Waldorf Towers. In the entry hall stood a John Singer Sargent portrait of George Washington, but the rest of the apartment was bare. Barbara faced the job of furnishing five bedrooms and a living room almost half the size of a football field. She borrowed furniture from the Waldorf Hotel, paintings from the Metropolitan Museum, and decorative glass objects from the Steuben Company.

The Metropolitan also sent her two paintings by French impressionist Claude Monet, which she returned to the museum. When criticized for rejecting a proud part of the Met's collection, she said, in typical straightforward Barbara fashion, "When the French start hanging American artists, I'll think about hanging French paintings." She knew that her job as the wife of the American ambassador was to put America on display, not France.

And put it on display they did. In addition to having parties at the apartment, they took foreign ambassadors on boat tours around Manhattan, to baseball games (a sport they found difficult to explain to foreigners seeing it for the first time), to movies, to lunches with their own family in Connecticut, to weekends in Kennebunkport—even to see NASA in Houston. Anytime they were not entertaining, they, in turn, were attending lunches and dinners and receptions, oftentimes several in one evening. Barbara said, "I loved all that. In fact, I was born to the job. I love people and adore eating."

She was also doing an important job for the future. During George's time as president of the United States, many years later, foreign leaders whom they had welcomed during their UN days took President Bush's calls readily, making cooperation between countries on world problems possible.

President Nixon disappointed Barbara when he asked George to leave the UN after two years and move back to Washington to be the chairman of the Republican National Committee. She knew he would have to travel constantly, mediating intraparty squabbles. It looked like a lonely time for her, a combative time for him, and a dead end politically. Always loyal to his party, though, George accepted the position.

Barbara did find some positives in the move. They could live in a house again rather than in a high-rise apartment, and Doro could be back in school with the friends with whom she had grown up. Neil moved home, and Marvin was nearby. Barbara basked in being with her children. On her forty-eighth birthday, the family thrilled her with the gift of a blond cocker spaniel puppy they named C. Fred (after a close friend). She resumed her busy schedule of belonging to women's organizations and working volunteer jobs and playing tennis, and every Sunday night they invited twelve to twenty-five people over for a cookout. Jeb, who was studying at the University of Texas at Austin, made them happy by marrying Columba, a young woman he had met during a high school program in Mexico. Columba spoke little English, and Barbara, remembering how intimidated she had been when she first met her own husband's family, did all she could to make Columba feel welcome, though Barbara spoke no Spanish.

George found the job as difficult as Barbara had feared as he tried to maneuver his party through the unfolding Watergate scandal, which resulted in Richard Nixon's resignation and Gerald Ford becoming president. As disheartening as this period was, Barbara felt that she had witnessed the greatness of a country in which the transition from one president to another happened smoothly.

Soon the Bushes moved again. President Ford asked George to take any ambassadorship he wanted, and George, passing over sought-out places like London and Paris, asked for the challenge of being chief of the US Liaison Office to the People's Republic of China. (There was no ambassador to that country at the time.) A shocked Barbara, who had never dreamed she would visit China, much less live there, adapted quickly to the idea and chose to think of it as an adventure and a chance to have George by her side instead of traveling all the time. Immediately, she began preparing by taking classes to learn the Chinese language.

All the children, including fifteen-year-old Doro, would remain in the United States, George at Harvard Business School, Jeb married and in Austin, Marvin at boarding school in Virginia, and Neil at Tulane University in Louisiana. Barbara's child-rearing days were winding down. Only Barbara, George, and C. Fred (and seventeen cases of dog food) would make the seven-thousand-mile trip to China. C. Fred proved to be a special comfort to them so far from home.

They arrived in Beijing to a residence whose staff spoke no English, and within an hour they were holding a reception for the fifty-three members of the liaison office. Quickly they fell into a routine. One of them walked C. Fred at about six o'clock each morning, they had yogurt for breakfast, listened to the Voice of America broadcaster on the radio (one of the few ways for them to get news), and worked until eleven o'clock, when a Chinese teacher helped them with the difficulties of the language. Then they ate lunch and worked again until dinner. At night they read Chinese history. At about 10:00 p.m., Barbara walked C. Fred again, feeling safe on the streets in their embassy neighborhood, although Chinese onlookers stared at them because China had few dogs and none with blond curls like C. Fred's. Barbara learned to say in Chinese, "Don't be afraid. He is a little dog. He doesn't bite people."

They bought bicycles on their first day in China, and Barbara continued to ride throughout George's ambassadorship. She found a friend to play tennis with. On Sundays, the family attended a Christian church with about twenty multinational parishioners muddling through a Chinese-language service and all singing the hymns in their own language. Many American guests visited the Bushes, including their children and President and Mrs. Ford. Barbara twice traveled seven thousand miles home to see her family, once for Christmas—the first time she and George had been separated for an extended time. Unbeknownst to her, George wrote a number of friends in Washington, asking them to keep her busy so she would not be lonely. Meanwhile, George's mother spent Christmas in China with him so he would not have to be alone for the holidays. Barbara also surprised Marvin at his high school graduation, which she couldn't bear for him to celebrate without a parent there.

Back in China, Barbara and George explored the country by train and by bicycle: dairy farms, Peking duck farms, the Great Wall of China, and the Forbidden City. They entertained frequently. Many details of this adventure are lost to us because Barbara became aware that the household staff were spying on them for the Chinese government, so she quit writing in her diary.

After fourteen months, in 1975, President Ford surprised them when he asked George to return to the United States to head up the Central Intelligence Agency (CIA). Barbara had made a home in China and learned a new culture, and once again she was being asked to leave it.

In Washington, as head of a spy agency, George could not talk about his work, and security measures for the Bushes were stringent. Several times they had to live with employees secretly and travel anonymously for their own safety.

Nevertheless, Barbara threw herself back into her former Washington life, volunteering and playing tennis. In addition, she made speeches and showed slides about China. But despite her busyness, she was unhappy. "It was the first time I'd ever been faced with nobody at home. I'd been such an active mother. And then such an active wife in China. Then suddenly, although George tried to include me at the CIA, there wasn't much I could be included in on. And I saw all these people out working in the man's world and suddenly thought, 'Well, gee, I should have done that?'" She said she "felt inadequate."

Barbara suffered depression during what she called her "wasted year." She talked to no one about it except George, and "many a time when he probably should have been asleep, he was holding me in his arms while I wept away." George suggested she get professional help, but she couldn't bring herself to do it. The experience left her with compassion for the many people who she knew also suffered silently, and she learned that people should feel freer than she had to get help for a condition they could not simply talk themselves out of. In her memoir, published many years later, she remembered that "sometimes the pain was so great, I felt the urge to drive into a tree or an oncoming car." Hearing this positive woman confess to such negativity has, no doubt, helped others to face their own dark thoughts with less shame and to obey her admonition to get help rather than to hide their condition.

Shortly, the Bushes' life took another major turn. In 1976 Jimmy Carter was elected president and wanted to appoint his own CIA director. George and Barbara returned to Houston. In the 1970s alone, the Bushes had lived in Washington, New York, Beijing, Washington again, and now Houston.

That, too, would last only a few years. George began traveling the country, laying the groundwork for his run at the presidency. When he announced his candidacy, Barbara became an active campaigner, crisscrossing the country on her own. She found that she had to prove herself as a person of substance and not a decoration to the campaign. She told of her hurt feelings when one national interviewer said that people were calling George a man of the 1980s and her a woman of the '40s. Lightly, she managed to reply, "Oh, you mean I look forty? Neat." She then went on to say, "If you mean that I love my God, my country, and my husband, so be it." She confessed that she had felt like crying upon hearing that comment aimed at her. She even had to defend her appearance when consultants suggested she make herself more stylish to appeal to the public. "I will do anything you want," she stated firmly, "but I won't dye my hair, change my wardrobe, or lose weight." "Barbara" was the person she was going to be.

During this period, Barbara identified what would become her life's passion. First Ladies traditionally promote a cause of particular concern to them. Barbara, as a candidate's wife, was asked what she would choose if George were elected. She pondered the question, deciding she wanted a project that would improve the lives of the greatest number of people while costing the government a modest amount. She selected literacy. Too many adults had no job because they could not read a help-wanted ad. Too many children failed in school because they had not conquered reading. She would try to help all ages with this most basic of skills. For the rest of her life, she spent her energy and money devoted to making readers of us all, with major success.

By the time of the Republican National Convention in 1980, George had the second-highest number of votes, but it was obvious that Ronald Reagan would be the Republican candidate for president. Barbara expected soon to return to Houston. Instead, Reagan chose Bush as his vice presidential running mate, and in a few more months, Barbara was living in the vice president's residence in Washington, a thirty-three-room Victorian mansion on ten acres of lawn. They remained there for the next eight years, the longest their family had lived in one place.

Barbara called these the busiest years of her life. The Bushes visited all fifty states, traveled to sixty-five foreign countries, hosted almost 1,200 events at the vice president's house, and attended over 1,200 other occasions in Washington. Two of their children, Marvin and Doro, married, and eight grandchildren were born. On the rare few nights they spent at home, they both took work upstairs after dinner—he to the second floor and she to the third. "We leave the doors open and yell," she told an interviewer.

On one of their trips to Japan—where George Bush had been shot down as a young pilot in World War II—she sat at lunch in the Imperial Palace next to Emperor Hirohito, who had been emperor during the war. Conversation faltered. The emperor answered her questions in one word and then sat silent. Searching for something to draw him out, Barbara remarked that she thought the palace was lovely and asked if it was new.

"Yes," was the monosyllabic answer.

"Was the old palace just so old it was falling down?" she asked, attempting to keep the conversation going.

"No," he replied, "I'm afraid that you bombed it."

She could find nothing more to say. She turned for conversation to the person sitting on her other side.

During the vice presidency, Barbara focused on making the country aware of the problem she had identified as her strong interest during the election: that of nonreaders being left behind. "Over forty million Americans cannot read," she said. "The inability to fill out an employment form, read a bus schedule, or interpret simple directions both embarrasses and isolates one in five Americans. . . . We must solve this problem." She made hundreds of speeches on the subject. She asked people to volunteer as reading teachers. She requested governors' wives to promote literacy in their states. She reminded communities to support their public libraries. She created the Barbara Bush Foundation for Family Literacy, and to fund it, she (and her dog) wrote a book entitled

C. Fred's Story by "C. Fred Bush edited slightly by Barbara Bush." She hoped to raise $25,000 from its sales. Instead, the book garnered $100,000 in profits and donations. (C. Fred, after having done this service for his country, died from a stroke.)

CHAPTER 5

PRESIDENCY

In 1988, George ran for president again. Again, Barbara packed her simple travel wardrobe of either black, blue, or brown so that she needed only one color of accessories. She made speeches, gave interviews, and smiled at rallies throughout the country, all the while despising the contentiousness of campaigns against candidates who otherwise would be their friends. To keep her spirits up, she stayed away from the nightly meetings of the staff to talk over the past day, and she did not watch the news on television. Listening to their campaign strategists worry about George's chances to win discouraged her. Hearing her husband's name tossed about carelessly or unfairly by news commentators pained her. Instead, she went to her room and read what she called "no-think" books.

George won the nomination of his party at the Republican National Convention in New Orleans in August 1988. It was a Bush family affair. The first day of the convention, Jeb's wife Columba—who had become an American citizen without telling the Bushes so she could surprise them at the convention—gave a second speech for her father-in-law, first in Spanish and then in English. Barbara said she was "bursting with pride." That night sixty-five members of the Bush family gathered for dinner together. A nervous and eager Barbara woke up the next morning at four o'clock. At a lunch given by the National Federation of Republican Women to honor her, daughter Doro introduced her, choking up as she said that her mother was a woman who "stands out like a beacon for those of us searching for real people." That night each child made the nomination of George Bush for their own state—Neil for Colorado; Jeb, Florida; Doro, Maine; George W., Texas; Marvin, Virginia; and George's sister, Nancy Ellis, Massachusetts. Then Barbara spoke about George. She began by telling the worldwide audience, "I've loved George Bush almost since the day I laid eyes on him." She ended by saying, "You've nominated for the presidency a man who is as strong and caring and decent as America herself."

For the next two months, they campaigned against Democratic Governor of Massachusetts Michael Dukakis. Barbara continued to despise unfair criticism aimed at George. She disliked it equally when those in her own party treated the opponent meanly, and she took them to task if they did. Fair play mattered to her.

On November 8, 1988, the Bushes voted in Houston at 7:40 in the morning. Sixty people were waiting in line at the polling place. They insisted the Bushes vote first. Then, the couple walked five miles in Memorial Park and looked for ways to fill their day. That night, at 8:16, George and Barbara Bush learned on CBS television that they were the new president and First Lady of the United States.

The night before the inauguration, six thousand people honored Barbara Bush at the Kennedy Center in its "Salute to the First Lady"—an evening of music ranging from performances by the National Symphony to mariachis singing

"Deep in the Heart of Texas" to Jeb and Columba's eleven-year-old daughter Noelle playing the accordion and presenting her grandmother with a white sombrero. In her own remarks, Barbara let it be known that the country could expect a down-to-earth First Lady when she said, "I want you all to look at me. Look at my hairdo, my makeup, my designer clothes. Take a good, long look at me this week. It's the last time you're going to see me like this."

The next morning, January 20, 1989, Barbara, in a turquoise wool coat, stood beside George, holding George Washington's Bible while her husband was sworn in as the forty-first president of the United States.

During the ceremony, moving vans removed the Reagans' possessions from the White House and replaced them with the Bushes'. That night, the Bush family, including the new First Lady and president, their children and spouses, and ten grandchildren, spent the night at 1600 Pennsylvania Avenue.

The next morning, thirty thousand people stood outside the White House and, when they saw the Bushes at the window, sang "God Bless America." Barbara called that the nicest moment of the inauguration.

The new First Lady soon discovered how contained her life would be. She and George could not walk to church two blocks away because crowds formed and traffic stopped. Nor could Barbara, in her bathrobe, let the dog out the back door in the morning. That chore required getting dressed and taking an elevator and walking past working crews and through long halls to get to the South Grounds. She could not fly on commercial airlines because required security searches of the plane would cause delays irritating to the passengers. The safety of the first family required that even their Kennebunkport house be closed in by a chain-link fence and trees be cut down in order to build a small house for a doctor and a military aide. The First Lady cried when she saw her ocean getaway penned in like a prison. Even here they were not free to walk to the corner store because the press followed and then asked the store clerks how much they had spent and what they had bought.

Other aspects of living in the White House delighted her. A staff of ninety-three people cared for them. She had a swimming pool and tennis courts, and they could eat off Abraham Lincoln's or Teddy Roosevelt's or Lady Bird Johnson's china. Each year their staff created a fairyland of decorated Christmas trees for them. Best of all, she and the president worked only rooms away from each other, and they often had lunch or took a break together to stroll around the lawn. "We always have lived in happy houses, but nothing matched this special place," she said.

Soon after the Bushes moved into the White House, Barbara developed Graves' disease, a thyroid condition that causes bulging eyes, periodic double vision, fatigue, and weight loss. She lost eighteen pounds in just three months and had to undergo radiation treatments on her thyroid. Mysteriously, George developed the same disease, and their dog a similar canine version. Nevertheless, she maintained her high-speed schedule, which included seventy-two laps daily in the pool and tennis several times a week. Yet, people continued to ask her how she felt when she would have preferred to talk about other things. One night, she and George were attending the annual journalists' Gridiron dinner with over six hundred guests. She knew that people would ask about her health, and she knew that in the skits, jokes would be made about her white hair. She decided to change the subject. She attended the dinner wearing a strawberry-blond wig—and stole the show. No one asked her how she felt, and they were unable to joke about her white hair.

As the First Lady, she found every day would erupt with even more activity than she had known as the wife of the vice president—or Second Lady—so much so that she now required her own office staff of fourteen people. In the first one hundred days alone, she gave seventy-nine parties at the White House, traveled to four countries and nine states, and met with the press twenty-four times. In the first year, she received 100,000 pieces of mail. She determined that as First Lady she would not waste her unique opportunity to make an impact for good. She told her staff that every day their goal would be to do something to help others. She contributed words or her presence to aid many ceremonial and nonprofit events: celebrating the one-hundredth anniversary of the National Zoo, lighting the national Christmas tree, throwing out the first pitch at a World Series game, holding and kissing babies with AIDS in order to demonstrate that it was not dangerous to do so, as many people still believed.

Meanwhile, she continued to care most about adults and children being able to read. By that time, she had studied the subject for ten years. As Second Lady, she had made the country aware of its literacy problem, and as First Lady she attacked it with the full force of her practical, energetic, and persistent personality. Her foundation published books telling states and individuals how they could help and gave money to those trying to start reading programs. She emphasized the importance of families reading together by having her own Sunday evening radio show, *Read Me a Story,*

Mrs. Bush visits Big Bird on the set of *Sesame Street*, October 1989. Courtesy of George H. W. Bush Presidential Library and Museum.

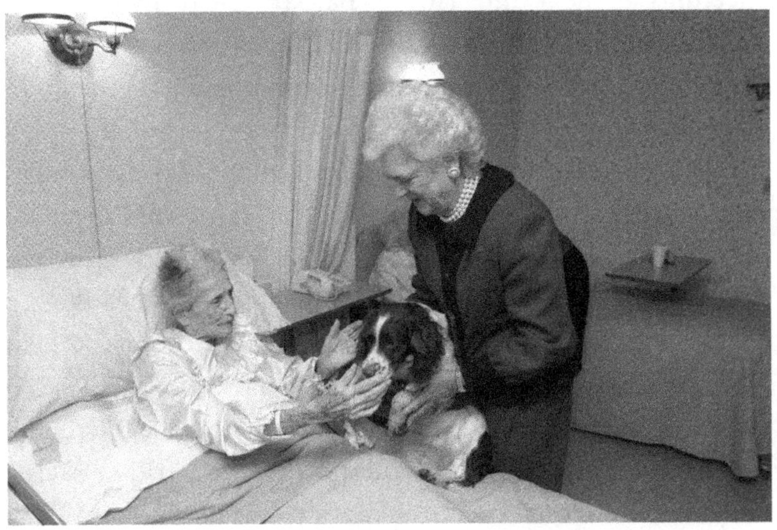

Mrs. Bush and her dog Millie visit a resident of a nursing home in Chevy Chase, Maryland, February 1990. Courtesy of George H. W. Bush Presidential Library and Museum.

in which she read to children. She raised more money by writing another book with another dog, *Millie's Book*, which made bestseller lists and brought in another $1 million to fund her foundation. She worked with Congress to get legislation passed to strengthen literacy programs. President Bush commented that she was "working her heart out for literacy." She continued to do so throughout her life, and this, her legacy, continues improving lives on her behalf today.

Each year the First Lady received at least a hundred invitations to speak at graduation ceremonies. She tried to accommodate as many schools as possible and to spread her appearances across the country. In the spring of 1990, she was scheduled to address the graduates at Wellesley College in Massachusetts. At the same time, Soviet leader Mikhail Gorbachev and his wife, Raisa, were in the United States for meetings at the White House. Barbara Bush invited Raisa Gorbachev to attend the Wellesley graduation with her: two of the most famous women in the world honoring the graduates of this one school.

Wellesley had chosen its graduation speaker by popular vote of the seniors. Their first choice was *The Color Purple* author and Pulitzer Prize winner Alice Walker, who declined the invitation. They invited their second choice, Barbara Bush.

Despite their classmates having already chosen the First Lady by vote in preference to other candidates such as Supreme Court Justice Sandra Day O'Connor and astronaut Sally Ride, 150 of the 600 seniors signed a petition saying they were "outraged" at the invitation because Barbara Bush had "gained recognition through the achievements of her husband, which contravenes what we've been taught over the last four years," and because she had dropped out of Smith College after two years to marry.

The country erupted in debate. The *Denver Post* called the protesters "snobbish little brats," while the all-male Harvard student newspaper vigorously supported the female protesters. Newspapers as far away as Australia commented. Obviously, both men and women wanted to clarify for themselves whether women's roles in the late twentieth century could and should be as passive observers of history or primary actors in history. Were you being passive if you did not follow a career? Were you being passive if you were not paid for your work?

Barbara Bush tried to keep the discussion civil. She said she could see the young women's point of view but thought that they misunderstood that she had chosen—not been forced into—her own "fabulously exciting, interesting, involved life." She even talked to one of the most outspoken student protesters, Christine Bicknell, to discuss their differences.

Barbara Bush and Raisa Gorbachev arrived at Wellesley on June 1, 1990. Five thousand people awaited them outside the tent where the graduation was to be held, and another five thousand awaited them inside.

At the beginning of her speech, Barbara Bush acknowledged the student protester Christine Bicknell as "my new best friend."

Then she addressed the controversy directly and with humor. "Now, I know," she said, "your first choice today was Alice Walker—guess how I know!—known for *The Color Purple*. Instead, you got me—known for the color of my hair."

She went on to tell them that, in their lives, as important

as their careers were going to be, they would not be more important than their human connections.

She acknowledged that they were living in a time of transition for women and men. And she counseled them that, no matter their successes, the success of their entire society depended "not on what happens at the White House, but what happens in your house." If they have children, those children must come first. They should be read to and hugged and loved.

She ended by saying, "Who knows? Somewhere out in this audience may even be someone who will one day follow in my footsteps, and preside over the White House as the president's spouse—and I wish him well."

The audience cheered. Some students had tears running down their cheeks. Tom Brokaw, on NBC News, pronounced it "one of the best commencement speeches I've ever heard."

Twenty-five years later, Christine Bicknell Marden, in the Wellesley alumna magazine, said that after graduation, "we really talked a lot about how much grace and class she had in delivering her speech which really focused on individual choices for women. . . . For a lot of us we have turned over that speech many times in the intervening years and taken away nuggets ever since."

Barbara Bush had offered the country three gold nuggets:

1. Deal with your opposition with kindness, with humor, and always with civility;
2. Both women and men can choose the role they prefer to play—careerist or homemaker—and both occupations are worthy;

3. Human connections to family and friends should be equal to your careers in importance.

Barbara Bush had no college degree when she addressed the graduates of Wellesley, but she was presented with thirty-one honorary degrees throughout her lifetime, twelve of which were awarded to her by 1990.

In August of 1990, Iraq invaded Kuwait in an attempt to seize its oil-rich lands. The world feared that Iraq's next victim would be Saudi Arabia, in which case it would control 40 percent of the world's oil supply. For six months, the United States and thirty-two other countries together demanded that Iraq withdraw from Kuwait. Then the US-led coalition invaded and pushed Iraq back across the border into its own country in a forty-two-day battle called the Gulf War. During that time, Barbara Bush took on the role of comforting young men and women in the military, as well as their families. In spite of a recent broken leg from a sledding accident, she traveled to nine military bases, assuring troops of their country's appreciation for the dangers they faced on its behalf. She recalled to them how she, too, as a young college girl, had awaited her fiancé, who was fighting in World War II in the Pacific.

She also warned parents throughout the country of the importance of talking to their children about what was happening in the war. The children were seeing the conflict on TV, and they, undoubtedly, were feeling fearful and needing the reassurance of adults. Always, she had families at the front of her mind.

And anyone who suffered. She told reporters that her

Mrs. Bush and daughter-in-law Laura Bush, a future First Lady, at a hospital for children with AIDS, Dallas, Texas, October 1991. Courtesy of George H. W. Bush Presidential Library and Museum

theme at commencement addresses that year would be tolerance. She knew that Arabs living in the US must be fearful of how Americans would treat them because of the war.

After the war, President and Mrs. Bush visited Kuwait at the invitation of that country's government, which wanted to express its gratitude. There they learned that a number of thankful Kuwaitis had named their newborns "Bush." Upon returning home, they found out that a plot for some Iraqis to bomb the Bushes' car while they were in Kuwait had been discovered and thwarted.

When the time came for reelection in 1992, George Bush and Arkansas Governor Bill Clinton faced each other. Barbara campaigned aggressively, making multiple speeches in multiple states on any given day. Wherever she went, she was well received, perhaps the most effective campaigner George Bush had. She tried to avoid discussing contentious issues, although interviewers sometimes attempted to force controversy into the conversation. Instead, she lauded her husband, explained why he should lead the country, and resorted to humor to get over a rough spot. In Texas, she traveled with her

Multiple generations of First Ladies (*left to right:* Lady Bird Johnson, Pat Nixon, Nancy Reagan, Mrs. Bush, Rosalynn Carter, and Betty Ford) in the courtyard of the Ronald Reagan Presidential Library, November 1991. Courtesy of George H. W. Bush Presidential Library and Museum.

Spanish-speaking grandson, George P. Bush, saying, "American issues are Hispanic issues, and Hispanic issues are American issues." In New Jersey, she said, "We don't need another Democrat governor promising another 'miracle.' We need George Bush's America!"

Early in the campaign, the Bushes traveled to Japan, shoring up the president's reputation as one who was skilled at foreign affairs. While there, Barbara took an unfortunate incident and turned it into a save. At a large dinner, the president—suddenly overcome with stomach flu—broke out in a cold sweat, vomited on the prime minister of Japan, and fell to the floor. After the president was carried off to his room, Prime Minister Miyazawa asked Mrs. Bush if she would like to say a few words. She was unprepared and worried about her husband. Uncertainly, she got up and thanked the Japanese for a wonderful visit. Then, drawing on her always-ready sense of humor, she said, "You know, I can't explain what happened to George because it never happened before, but I'm beginning to think it's the ambassador's fault. He and George played the emperor and crown prince in tennis today, and they were badly beaten. And we Bushes aren't used to that. So he felt much worse than I thought." In relief, the audience laughed and relaxed.

"Sometimes," Barbara Bush said, "the campaign took a definite turn for the silly," as when the Wellesley debate about women erupted again. This time, however, it was precipitated by the traditional wives who felt that those—such as Hillary Rodham Clinton—who had chosen careers treated them insensitively.

Candidate Clinton's wife, Hillary Rodham Clinton, a generation younger than Barbara Bush, was asked in an interview if she had done the wrong thing to practice law while her husband was governor. She responded, "I suppose I could have stayed home and baked cookies and had teas, but what I decided to do was fulfill my profession." Just as career women had attacked Barbara Bush before her Wellesley speech for not being their kind of woman, now a storm of criticism rained down on Hillary Clinton from stay-at-home wives, who thought Clinton was belittling them.

The magazine *Family Circle* seized the moment to declare a cookie bake-off between the two candidates' wives, neither of whom claimed to be a cookie baker. It published Hillary Clinton's recipe for oatmeal cookies with chocolate chips and Barbara Bush's chocolate chip cookies without oatmeal and asked readers to vote. The Clinton cookies won 55 percent to Bush's 45 percent.

Barbara Bush wrote in her diary that her office had known nothing about the contest until her recipe was published in the magazine—and it wasn't her recipe. The magazine had used one published when the Bushes lived in the vice president's house, and the recipe had belonged to their chef. Subsequently, Barbara Bush published her own version, which includes oatmeal.

The spouses' baking contest in *Family Circle* became a permanent part of presidential campaigns. Over twenty years after the first one, when Hillary Clinton was a candidate for president herself, Bill Clinton submitted the same chocolate chip cookie recipe his wife had in 1992. It won over Melania Trump's sugar cookies cut in the shape of stars.

Barbara and George rarely got to travel together. Often she went to sleep in a hotel room at night, watching George on the television in another part of the country.

Adding to her busy campaign schedule, she tried to visit literacy programs, especially when she could read to children. (Her campaign staff reminded her that children could not vote, but this was too important to her to give up.) In one week alone, she spoke in eleven cities in seven states, at eight fundraisers, five literacy events, and three rallies. She traveled by bus, plane, car, and train.

In the end, George Bush lost the election, primarily because Americans were disappointed in their sluggish economy.

CHAPTER 6

THE BUSH CHILDREN

By the time Barbara and George Bush left the presidency, George W., Jeb, Neil, Marvin, and Doro were established in their adult lives. Let us pause here to review their journeys.

Each was named after a family member or a close friend, and each had a nickname within the family. Barbara was known as the Enforcer or the Silver Fox, and George as Poppy.

GEORGE WALKER BUSH

Named after his father
Nickname: Georgie, until he became president and said to his mother, "I bet George Washington's mother didn't call him Georgie." Then, he and his father became "41" and "43" in the family, a reference to their being the forty-first and forty-third presidents of the United States.

George, the oldest, resembled his mother in personality but lived a life that reenacted that of his father in important ways. He had his mother's exuberant and informal personality, quick to make a quip or to voice his opinion. They loved

President and Mrs. Bush with their grandchildren at Camp David, Thurmont, Maryland, September 1992. Courtesy of George H. W. Bush Presidential Library and Museum.

to tease each other and the rest of the family. Like his father, he went to Andover in Massachusetts for high school and to Yale for college, although he was not the student his father was. He went on to get a master's degree in business at Harvard, and then he, like his father, drove to Midland and tried to find a way into the oil business. While there, he met and married Laura Welch when they were both thirty and set behind him a lively partying life and a rebellious streak that had sometimes put him at odds with his parents. He, like his father, became interested in politics and ran for Congress, although unsuccessfully. Also like his father, he loved baseball and put together a group of investors to buy the Texas Rangers baseball team in Arlington. And, of course, he became governor of Texas and then president of the United States, the only son of a president in American history to follow his father into office since the second and sixth presidents, John Adams and John Quincy Adams.

Like her mother-in-law, Laura Bush, a former public school librarian, advocated for education and literacy when she was First Lady. She established the National Book Festival, which is still attended by 120,000 people a year.

JOHN ELLIS BUSH

Named for his uncle, John Ellis, married to George H. W. Bush's sister, Nancy
Nickname: Jeb, for his three initials, J.E.B.

Jeb, seven years younger than George, followed his brother and father to Andover. In his senior year of high school, he went to Mexico on a work-study program. He fell in love with Columba Garnica de Gallo there in the same immediate, head-over-heels way his father had when he met Barbara. He also fell in love with Mexico and, rather than follow family tradition by attending Yale, got a degree in Latin American studies at the University of Texas at Austin. When he was twenty-one, he and Columba married, and, after a career in real estate development in Florida, Jeb won the Florida governorship, which he held for eight years. In 2015 and 2016, he made an unsuccessful attempt to be the Republican nominee for president of the United States.

NEIL MALLON BUSH

Named after a Bush family friend, Neil Mallon, who encouraged the young Bushes to move to Odessa, Texas, and work for his company, Dresser Industries
Nickname: Whitey because of his blond hair, then Whitney, and finally, Whit

Neil, the third son, had difficulty reading as a child, and in second grade, he was diagnosed with dyslexia, which was not studied much at that time. Barbara refused to believe his teachers' warnings that he would not succeed in college. She read to him and with him and encouraged him to persist in school. This bright young man ended up with a bachelor's degree and a master's degree from Tulane University. He and his wife, Maria, met in Houston when she worked at the Barbara Bush Houston Literacy Foundation. After his mother's death, Neil continued her work by heading up the foundation.

MARVIN PIERCE BUSH

Named after Barbara's father
Nickname: Marty

In a large family with three older brothers to compete with, Marvin said that he never felt pressure from his parents to be someone he was not. "That, to me, is one of their greatest accomplishments. All their children are extremely different, and they appreciate us for who we are."

Because she had ovarian cancer as a young woman, his wife, Margaret, could not have children, so the couple adopted two babies. After graduating from the University of Virginia, Marvin developed life-threatening ulcerative colitis at age twenty-nine while George Bush was vice president. Optimistic by nature, like his mother, he has learned to live fully in spite of his health and has given much of his time to encouraging others with the same disease, an activity he said thrilled his mother. Marvin has also had a successful career in financial management.

DOROTHY WALKER BUSH KOCH

Named after George H. W.'s mother
Nickname: Doro

After President Bush's retirement, Doro, who was exceptionally close to her father, wrote a nearly six-hundred-page book about his life, doing considerable research. Like her mother, she was not strongly inclined to a career, but she did earn a degree in sociology from Boston College. In order to assist her father with his first presidential campaign, she took courses in shorthand and typing so she could help in his campaign office. She and her first husband had two children, then divorced, and she moved to Washington, DC, to be near her parents. Later, she married Bobby Koch at Camp David and had two more children.

CHAPTER 7
RETIREMENT

Barbara Bush said she felt a "deep fatigue" for two months following the 1992 election as they prepared to leave Washington for good. Everything they did had a "This is the last time we will ever do this" feeling. They took one last presidential trip to Russia. They said teary goodbyes to Washington friends. Barbara showed Hillary Clinton through the mansion and flew to Houston to look for a house of her own (after seeing twenty-two houses that she didn't want to live in, she decided they should build). They spent one last fairytale Christmas in the White House. During this period, they lost a beloved family member when George's mother died.

On January 20, 1993, George and Barbara Bush left behind the pageantry and the power and the problems of the president and First Lady and returned to private life. They carried with them a gift from the White House staff: the flag that had flown over the White House the day they had arrived and the flag that flew there the day they left.

Their first year back in Houston, Barbara wrote a memoir of her life up until 1994 and took it on a national book tour. She and George began planning the construction of the George Bush Presidential Library on the campus of

Texas A&M University in College Station. At the same time, the Bushes rented a house while building another one two doors away, and Barbara relearned how to shop, cook, and drive, which she had not done for twelve years. "I'm a better driver than cook," she said. In the family's teasing way, George, during a family spaghetti supper, remarked of her long-neglected cooking, "I like my pasta rare."

Near the end of that year, in an interview with Larry King, she said, "I loved living in the White House, but I don't miss it." With her typical practical nature, Barbara Bush had relished one segment of her life, then quickly moved on to the next with equal enthusiasm.

Ten years later she published a book about their retirement. Clearly, those years equaled the White House in nonstop activity. Even though the Bushes had crossed the finish line, they raced ahead like horses still in the homestretch, not to compete, but because they loved running. They spent part of the year in Houston and part in Kennebunkport, interspersed with frequent trips throughout the world and always surrounded by friends, family, and dignitaries.

Operating from their home bases of Houston and Kennebunkport, the Bushes' lives could be divided into big chunks of volunteer work, politics, receiving honors, travel, health, and entertaining as if they had more than the usual twenty-four hours in each day. "Sometimes," Barbara said, "I find retirement so exhausting that I think I'll get a job."

Her volunteer work continued unabated, always with literacy events at the forefront. She particularly enjoyed the annual evenings called A Celebration of Reading, sponsored by her foundation. These fundraisers consisted of dinner plus famous authors reading from their own books. By 2017, over sixty of these events had entertained contributors throughout the country, a pleasant way to raise millions of dollars for the cause of literacy and a joy to Barbara, who was reading most of these authors herself.

Her other most serious volunteer commitment was serving on the board of the Mayo Clinic Foundation in St. Paul, Minnesota. Wherever she was in the world, she always came home for a Mayo board meeting.

Politics was in the Bush blood. Before long, it captured another generation. George W. ran for governor of Texas and Jeb for governor of Florida—in the same year. Barbara campaigned for them and agonized over them and over the meanness in elections. Many times people asked her, "Is it harder for you when you and your husband run for office or when your son does?" The answer was always the same: "OUR SON." Even so, she was proud that her children were addressing, through politics, the issues of the day. One questioner remarked to Barbara how many sacrifices the family of a politician had to make and how much criticism they had to endure, and asked her how she felt when not one but two of her children chose this hard life. Her reply was strong: "I knew we had done something right." George was elected governor of Texas. Jeb was defeated for governor of Florida, but two years later he ran again and succeeded. Her sons were governors of the second and eighth most populated states, and Barbara mused, "Suddenly, one out of every eight Americans was governed by one of our sons!" In 2001, Barbara and George Bush attended the inauguration of George W. as president of the United States. He swore his oath on the same Bible his father had twelve years before. Barbara lived to see

Jeb as a candidate for the Republican primary for president and her grandson George P. (son of Jeb and Columba) also enter elective politics in Texas.

Honors rained on her. Particularly, the city of Houston appreciated her and named dog parks and schools after her. All the rest of her life, she could be seen walking one of her dogs, with a Secret Service agent following her, in Millie Bush Bark Park or the Bibi and Mini-Me Bush Dog Park (named for her Maltipoos). And as late as 2006, she was still listed in Gallup Poll's list of Most Admired Women.

The Bushes continued to travel for pleasure as well as for volunteer work and for speechmaking. (In one year alone, Barbara made seventy-nine speeches.) Bush spotters could find them throughout the world. One week Barbara would be seen with George in Sea Island, Georgia, celebrating their wedding anniversary. Another week, she would be seen with children and grandchildren, sailing the Greek isles. Or with friends, flying in hot-air balloons in Kenya. She might be seen alone, accompanying a planeload of medical supplies to Croatia, or again with George, petting Queen Elizabeth's Welsh corgis in Buckingham Palace.

Still in good health, she nevertheless had to stop several times those first ten years for surgery. She had two hip replacements, back surgery for sciatica, and two toes removed. George said she had been a perfect 10 before that operation but was now only an 8. She was experiencing the problems of aging.

Barbara and George both thrived on entertaining, which particularly occupied their summers in Kennebunkport. They slept thirty-four guests there and loved to keep the beds full. One year they had 178 people spend the night with them at Walker's Point, some staying for long periods. Organized Barbara handled a crowded household well, but she did occasionally lose patience. "Our 'grands' are driving us crazy," she wrote, "by

1. Opening the deep freeze for ice creams and Klondike Bars and leaving it open. Yikes;
2. They drink soft drinks and don't finish them. Every time I empty an almost full can I could choke them!!!"

From 1993 to 2018—for twenty-four years—their life followed this general pattern, slowing but not stopping. Then, at age ninety-two, suffering from congestive heart failure and chronic obstructive pulmonary disease, Barbara Bush died at home with George, her husband of seventy-three years, holding her hand.

After a service at St. Martin's Episcopal Church in Houston, her funeral motorcade passed one last time through a park where she had walked her dogs all those years and continued on to the George H. W. Bush Presidential Library and Museum at Texas A&M University in College Station, where she was buried next to daughter Robin, whose body had been moved there to rest beside her parents.

Today, at Barbara Bush Elementary School, in Houston, she is remembered every Friday, when more than eight hundred children sing:

Barbara Bush is our school's name,
From a grand First Lady it came.

Our school puts us to the test,
Helping us to do our best.
To our school we'll always be true,
Barbara Bush, we're proud of you,
Proud of you.

APPENDIX

Barbara Bush's Chocolate Chip Cookies

Ingredients

1 cup all-purpose flour
1 teaspoon baking soda
1 teaspoon salt
1 cup (2 sticks) unsalted butter, softened
1 cup sugar
1 cup light brown sugar
2 eggs
2 teaspoons vanilla extract
2 cups quick-cooking oats (not instant)
1 (12-ounce) package semisweet chocolate chips

Directions

Heat oven to 350°F. Sift together flour, baking soda, and salt onto waxed paper. Set aside. Beat together butter, granulated sugar, brown sugar, eggs, and vanilla in a large bowl until fluffy. Stir in flour mixture until well blended. Stir in oats and chocolate chips. Drop batter by rounded tablespoonfuls, 2 inches apart, onto ungreased cookie sheets. Bake at 350°F for 10 minutes, or until lightly browned. Transfer cookies to wire rack to cool.

Hillary Clinton's Chocolate Chip Cookies

Ingredients

1½ cups unsifted all-purpose flour
1 teaspoon salt
1 teaspoon baking soda
1 cup solid vegetable shortening
1 cup firmly packed light brown sugar
½ cup granulated sugar
1 teaspoon vanilla extract
2 eggs
2 cups rolled old-fashioned oats
1 (12-ounce) package semisweet chocolate chips

Directions

Heat oven to 350°F. Grease two large baking sheets. Combine flour, salt, and baking soda on a sheet of parchment or waxed paper. In a large bowl, beat together the shortening, sugars, and vanilla with an electric mixer until creamy. Add eggs, beating until light and fluffy. Gradually beat in flour mixture and rolled oats. Stir in chocolate chips. Drop batter by well-rounded teaspoonfuls onto prepared sheets. Bake at 350°F for 8 to 10 minutes or until golden. Cool cookies on sheets for 2 minutes. Remove to wire rack to cool completely.

LETTER FROM GEORGE BUSH

George Bush was asked to write about his favorite authors for a fundraiser for a literacy program. This is what he wrote:

Dear Reader,
This is a letter about two of the great authors I have known and loved.

The first, our dog Millie. I used to be President of the USA. Millie, young and fast, lived in the White House. She chased squirrels on the White House lawn. She ran like a dart through the lovely woods at Camp David and climbed, sure-footedly on the rocks at Maine. She wrote a best selling book, ably assisted by my wife. Then this summer she got cancer and died and we wept.

The second author is Barbara Pierce Bush, the one who helped Millie write. Barbara is my wife—has been for almost 53 years. She wrote a *Memoir.* She helps our country know the importance of reading. She is down to earth. She loves grandkids, gardens, and dogs. She is a grand writer, but not scary like some authors. We laugh a lot together. We cry, too. We are two people, but we are one. I love her a lot.

Sincerely,
George Bush

NOTE TO THE BUSH CHILDREN AND GRANDCHILDREN

Barbara Bush posted this note on the back of the bedroom doors at Kennebunkport:

Children and Grandchildren

1. Please hang up damp towels and use twice if possible.
2. Try to make beds and keep room picked up . . . makes dusting and vacuuming easier.
3. Please collect your gear from around the house and keep it in your room.
4. If possible let the kitchen know your meal plans:
   —picnics
   —specific requests for you or your children
   —missing a meal.
5. Breakfast served from 8 to 9 a.m.—coffee beginning at 6:30 a.m.
   [It's really more like 5:30 a.m.!]
6. Please put dirty clothes outside your door every night.
7. Ask Paula if you can help her.
8. Above all—have a great time! This is our happiest time of the year!

SELECTED BIBLIOGRAPHY

Bush, Barbara. *A Memoir.* Charles Scribner's Sons, 1994.

Bush, Barbara. *Reflections: Life After the White House.* Scribner, 2003.

Bush, C. Fred *C. Fred's Story: A Dog's Life.* Edited slightly by Barbara Bush. Doubleday, 1984.

Bush, Millie. *Millie's Book*, as dictated to Barbara Bush. Harper Perennial, 1992.

Gutin, Myra G. *Barbara Bush: Presidential Matriarch.* University Press of Kansas, 2008.

Kilian, Pamela. *Barbara Bush: A Biography.* St. Martin's Press, 1992.

Radcliffe, Donnie. *Simply Barbara Bush: A Portrait of America's Candid First Lady.* Warner Books, 1989.

A profitable way to gain insight into Barbara Bush is to view her interviews online, especially with Larry King in 1994 and with Jenna Bush Hager in 2015.

www.ingramcontent.com/pod-product-compliance
Lightning Source LLC
LaVergne TN
LVHW041153200825
818805LV00008B/50

* 9 7 8 1 4 7 7 3 3 2 0 5 4 *